COOL JOBS

for

Young Pet Lovers

Ways to Make Money Caring for Pets

Pam Scheunemann

ABDO
Publishing Company

Visit us at www.abdopublishing.com

Published by ABDO Publishing Company, 8000 West 78th Street, Edina, Minnesota 55439.

Printed in the United States , North Mankato, Minnesota
052010
092010

 PRINTED ON RECYCLED PAPER

Design and Production: Kelly Doudna, Mighty Media, Inc.
Series Editor: Liz Salzmann
Photo Credits: Kelly Doudna, Shutterstock
Money Savvy Pig® photo courtesy of Money Savvy
Generation/www.msgen.com

**Library of Congress
Cataloging-in-Publication Data**

Scheunemann, Pam, 1955-
  Cool jobs for young pet lovers : ways to make money caring for pets / Pam Scheunemann.
     p. cm. -- (Cool kid jobs)
  Includes index.
  ISBN 978-1-61613-200-2
  1. Money-making projects for children--Juvenile literature.
2. Pet sitting--Vocational guidance--Juvenile literature. 3. Success in business--Juvenile literature. 4. Finance, Personal --Juvenile literature. I. Title.
  HF5392.S348 2011
  636.088'7023--dc22
                            2010004314

NOTE TO ADULTS

A job can be a good learning experience for you and your child. Be sure to encourage your child to discuss his or her job ideas with you. Talk about the risks and the benefits. Set up some rules for your child's safety with regard to:

* working with strangers

* transportation to and from the job

* proper and safe use of tools or equipment

* giving out phone numbers or e-mail addresses

* emergency contacts

Contents

Why Work?

There are a lot of reasons to have a job. The first one you probably think of is to earn money. But you can get more out of a job than just money. You can learn new skills, meet new people, and get some experience.

MAKING MONEY

When you do a job such as dog walking, or cat sitting, you are providing a service. If people pay you for your service, you can earn some money!

BESIDES MONEY

You will gain more than money from having a job. You also get work experience and learn about being responsible. That means showing up on time, keeping your word, and being trustworthy.

Volunteering is doing a job you don't get paid for. But you can earn other rewards. You can learn new skills that will help you get other jobs. And you can feel good about helping out!

What Can You Do with Your Money?

There are four things you can do with the money you earn.

SAVE

Saving is keeping your money in a safe place. You add money a little at a time as you earn it. Soon you could save enough for something such as a new bike.

SPEND

Spending is using your money to buy things you want. Maybe you want to go to a movie or buy a new computer game.

DONATE

It is important to give some of your earnings to organizations that help others.

INVEST

Investing is saving for long-term goals such as college expenses.

Ask your parents to help you decide how much money to use for each purpose. You'll be glad you did!

Money Savvy Pig®

What's Your Plan?

Each state has laws about kids working. If you are too young to work at a regular job, you can create your own job. Whatever job you try, you should have a plan.

WHAT WILL YOU DO?

Your job should relate to your likes and abilities. Make a list of the kinds of animals you like and know how to take care of. What's your favorite? Then think of what kinds of help pet owners might need.

WHO ARE YOUR CUSTOMERS?

Who needs your product or service? Where will you find your customers? How will you let people know about your services?

WHERE WILL YOU DO THE WORK?

Will you work at your house, the customers' homes, or another location?

SETTING REALISTIC GOALS

A goal is something you are working toward. When you set your job goals, keep these things in mind:

* Do you have permission from your parents?

* Is your idea something you already know how to do?

* Will this job interfere with your schoolwork or other activities?

* Are there any costs to start your job? Do you have the money or do you need to get a loan?

* Are there tools or **materials** you need to start your job? Will you continue to need supplies?

* Will you work alone or with a friend? How will you divide the work and the money you make?

What If It Doesn't Work?

Don't get **discouraged** if things don't work out the way you planned. Think about what you could have done differently and try again!

Get Permission

You must get permission from a parent or **guardian** before you work for someone else. Give your parents all of the details about the job.

WHO WILL YOU BE WORKING FOR?

Are you working for a relative or friend of the family? If not, your parents should meet your customer.

WHEN WILL YOU BE WORKING?

What day will you start the work? What time? Will your services be needed once or more often?

WHERE IS THE JOB?

Be sure your family has the address and phone number of where you are working. Create a Customer Information form similar to the one on page 15. Fill out a form for each customer.

HOW WILL YOU GET THERE?

Is your job within walking or biking distance? Do you need a ride there? Is it okay for you to take the bus to get there? What if it's during the evening or after dark?

WHO ELSE WILL BE THERE?

Are you going to do the job alone or with a friend? Will there be other people around while you are working?

WHAT IS EXPECTED OF YOU?

Are you clear about the job you were hired to do? Have you made an agreement with the customer about what is expected of you (see page 14)?

Be Smart, Be Safe

Talk with your parents about working for strangers. Always tell your parents where you are going and what time they should expect you to be home. Make sure they have a phone number where they can reach you while you are working.

ANIMAL SAFETY

Make sure you meet the pet and its owner before you start any job. You need to feel comfortable being in control of the animal. Let the animal get used to you. Always get the phone number for the veterinarian and another adult to call in case of an **emergency**.

If an animal that usually stays inside gets out of the house, get help right away. If an animal looks or acts strangely, ask for help. Animals can't tell you they are sick. It's up to you to notice any unusual behavior. It may not have anything to do with how you cared for the animal.

Getting the Word Out

Okay, you've decided what to do. Now how do you get the work? There are different ways to get the word out.

BUSINESS CARDS

A simple business card can be very helpful in getting customers. Give cards to the people you talk to about your business. Maybe even give each person an extra so he or she can pass one along to a friend.

Your business card should have your name, your business name, and your phone number. Get permission from a parent before putting your home address, phone number, or e-mail address on a card.

WORD OF MOUTH

Let as many people know about your business as you can. They'll tell other people, and those people will tell more people, and so on.

Four Paws
Pet Service

Josh Smith
123 Elm Street
Great Falls, MT 5940[...]
(406) 555-0145

Make Your Own Business Cards

PRO TIP
Use the computer to make your flyer and cards. Or, follow the steps here and on page 13 for a more personal touch.

1 On a piece of white paper, draw a rectangle with a black pen. It should be 3½ x 2 inches (9 x 5 cm). Design your business card inside the rectangle.

2 Make 11 copies of the card. Cut each one out, including the original. Cut outside the border so the lines show.

3 Tape the cards onto a piece of 8½ x 11-inch (22 x 28 cm) paper. Leave a ¼-inch (½ cm) border around the edge of the paper. This is your business card **master**.

4 Copy the master onto card stock. If you're using a black-and-white copier, try using colored card stock. Or, use white card stock and add color with markers or colored pencils.

5 Cut out your business cards. When you run out of cards, make more copies of your master.

WHAT YOU'LL NEED

white paper	tape
ruler	card stock (white or colored)
black pen	
copier	markers or colored pencils
scissors	

Four Paws Pet Service

We can help!

* Dog walking
* Pet sitting
* Dog brushing or bathing
* Yard or kennel clean-up

Call Josh Smith at (406) 555-0145
* Reasonable rates
* Lots of experience

Four Paws Pet Service (406) 555-0145

A flyer is a one-page sheet about your product or service. You can include more information than will fit on a business card. Make little mini cards at the bottom of the flyer for people to tear off. Include your service and phone number. Get your parent's permission first! Give flyers to people you know. Also, some places have bulletin boards for flyers:

* apartment building lobbies
* stores
* community centers
* schools
* places of worship

Make Your Own Flyer

1. Design a **master** copy of your flyer on a sheet of white paper that is 8½ x 11 inches (22 x 28 cm).

2. Use bright colors so your flyer will stand out. If you plan to use a black-and-white copier, use black on the master, and copy it onto colored paper.

3. Remember that copiers won't copy anything written too close to the edge of the master. So leave a border of at least ¼ inch (½ cm) on all sides.

4. Make as many copies of the master as you need. Cut the lines between the mini cards so customers can tear them off easily.

WHAT YOU'LL NEED

white paper

black pen

ruler

markers or colored pencils

copier

colored paper (optional)

scissors

Money Matters

One reason to work is so you can make money!

Here are some hints about money.

🐾 Four Paws Customer Agreement

Customer Name _____

Address _____

Phone_____
Job Description _____

Start Date_____ End Date _____

🐾 Schedule

MONDAY	TUESDAY	WEDNESDAY	THURSDAY	FRIDAY	SATURDAY	SUNDAY

🐾 Rate/Payment Agreement

Customer agrees to pay Four Paws Pet Service $_____
for the services listed above in the job description for each
[visit, day, week, month].

Payments will be made on a [per visit, weekly, monthly] basis.

_____ Date
Customer Signature

🐾 Four Paws Pet Service
Josh Smith, 123 Elm Street, Great Falls, MT 59404
(406) 555-0145

HOW MUCH SHOULD YOU CHARGE?

Here are things to consider when figuring out what to charge.

* Find out what other people charge for the same product or service.

* Are you providing tools or supplies? Make sure you charge enough to cover your costs.

* Do you want to charge by the hour or by the job? Will you charge less if they are steady customers?

MAKE AN AGREEMENT

Be clear with your customer about how much you are charging. Discuss the details with the customer.

Four Paws Customer Information

Customer:	
Address:	
Phone Number:	
Pet Name(s):	
Emergency Phone Numbers:	
Owner:	
Neighbor:	
Vet:	

House Information (keys, locks, security system, flashlights, fire extinguisher, etc.):

Pet Supply Information
(food, water, brushes, leashes, trash bags, cleaning supplies, etc.):

Pet Care Instructions:

Feeding (Where is the food? How much food? How often? When? Treats?):

Care (Medication? Walk or run? How much play time? Brushing? Bathing?):

Clean Up Details (Where is the trash? Litter box details? Other clean up?):

Pet Details (Habits, likes, dislikes, health issues, other?):

Four Paws Pet Service
Josh Smith, 123 Elm Street, Great Falls, MT 59404
(406) 555-0145

Sample form: make yours fit your business!

Then write them down on a Customer Agreement form. You and the customer should each have a copy of the Agreement.

Fill out a Customer Information form for each customer. Keep them in a folder with the Customer Agreements. Update the forms if anything changes.

HOW MUCH

DID YOU MAKE?

Profit is the amount of money you have left after you subtract your expenses. If you are only charging for your time, it's all profit, right? Not so fast! Did you have to make flyers or business cards? Did you provide supplies to do the job?

Add up your expenses. Subtract the expenses from the amount you earned. The amount left over is your profit.

Willing Dog Walker

If you like dogs, dog walking is a great way to make money. There are probably plenty of people in your neighborhood who have dogs. Many people don't have time to walk their dogs as often as they would like.

WHAT YOU'LL NEED

2 or 3 plastic bags

a leash

water for yourself and the dog (if you are going on a long walk)

BEFORE YOU BEGIN

Meet with your customer and the dog. You and your customer should walk the dog together the first time. That way you can see how the dog behaves on a walk. Fill out a Customer Agreement form (see page 14). Write down all the details for the job.

What time should the dog be walked? Should it be at the same time every day?

How long should the walks be? This may depend on the age and size of the dog.

Where should you walk the dog? There may be a park or special area for pet exercise nearby.

The dog should walk without pulling hard on the leash. Do a little research about the proper way to walk a dog.

Will your customer give you a key to the house? Or will a key be hidden somewhere? If they give you a key, label it with the customer's name. Keep it in a place where it won't get lost.

ON THE JOB

* When you walk the dog, stay on the sidewalk. If there isn't a sidewalk, stay as close to the curb as possible. Walk on the left side, so you can see cars coming.

* The dog will probably want to sniff everything. That's okay! But don't let the dog pull you all over the place! Remember, you are in charge.

* If it's really hot, let the dog rest in the shade occasionally. Have water available for the dog to drink.

* Be sure to pick up after the dog. Turn a plastic bag inside out over your hand. This way you can pick up the waste without getting dirty. Put the bag in a trash can.

Clean Dog, Happy Dog!

Dogs can get pretty dirty and smelly. People prefer petting a clean dog that doesn't smell bad. You can help make that a reality with your own dog washing service!

WHAT YOU'LL NEED

washtub

water

dog brush

dog shampoo/special "no tears" shampoo

lots of old towels

hair dryer (optional)

BEFORE YOU BEGIN

First you need to get clients for your dog washing business. Try having a special "Dog Wash" event where people bring their dogs to you.

Research the proper way to wash a dog. Even if you think you know how, you'll learn some new tips!

Make signs and advertise a week or two before the day of the Dog Wash.

Figure out how much to charge. Have change available.

Have plenty of dog shampoo and towels available. You may need special "no tears" shampoo for the dogs' faces.

If there is an electrical outlet nearby, you could also use a hair dryer for the finishing touch.

ON THE JOB

* Wear old clothes or a swimming suit. You're going to get wet!

* Brush the dog first. This gets rid of extra fur and makes washing easier.

* It might be helpful to have a dry friend help collect the money. The friend could also sell lemonade or snacks to the customers while they wait!

* Hand out business cards or flyers. People can get in touch with you for more work. Have a mailing list sign up form. Then you can send them information about future dog washes.

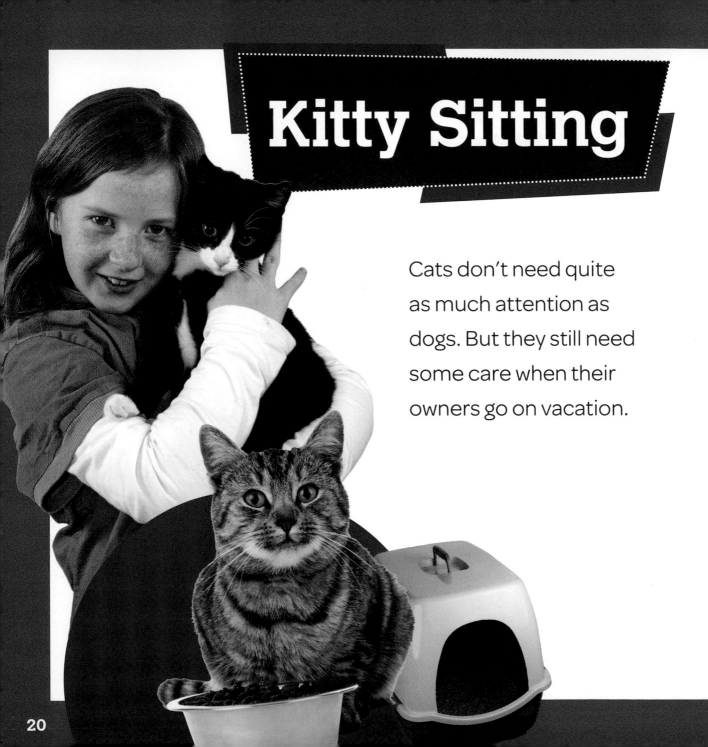

Kitty Sitting

Cats don't need quite as much attention as dogs. But they still need some care when their owners go on vacation.

BEFORE YOU BEGIN

Meet with your customer and the cat. Discuss how often you will need to check on the cat. Fill out a Customer Agreement form (see page 14). Write down all the details for the job.

Where is the cat food? How much should you feed it? How often?

Where is the litter box? How often should you scoop it? Where should you **dispose** of the dirty litter?

Will your customer give you a key to the house? Or will a key be hidden somewhere? If they give you a key, label it with the customer's name. Keep it in a place where it won't get lost.

WELL DONE
Save up for a giant cat play tower for your own cat!

ON THE JOB

If the cat eats wet food and there is some left in the bowl, throw it away. Rinse out the bowl. Make sure you feed the cat the right amount.

* Empty the water bowl and clean it thoroughly. Refill it with fresh water.

* Check the litter box. Follow the owner's instructions for taking care of it.

* Spend some time with the cat. See if it wants to play. Maybe it just wants to curl up in your lap!

Lizards, Hamsters, and Snakes, Oh My!

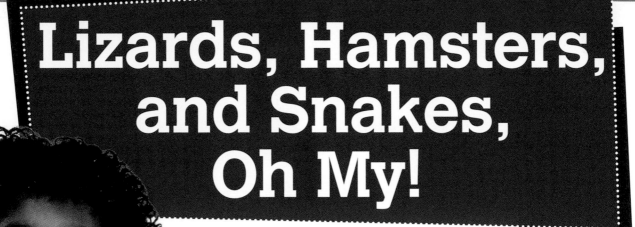

Not everyone has a dog or a cat. People have all sorts of pets. These pets also need care when their owners are out of town.

BEFORE YOU BEGIN

Meet with your customer and the pet. Discuss exactly what you need to do to take care of the animal. Fill out a Customer Agreement form (see page 14). Write down all the details for the job.

What kind of food does the animal eat? How much should you give it?

Is it okay to take the pet out of its cage to play?

Has the pet ever tried to escape? How do you keep it from escaping?

Some reptiles have hot rocks or special lights in their tanks. Be sure you know how to use the equipment properly.

If there is bedding in the cage, how often should you change it?

DO GOOD
Help pets in need! Donate some of your earnings to a local animal shelter.

ON THE JOB

Ask about feeding treats to the pet. Be sure to use the right treat for the pet. A treat for a hamster might not be good for another kind of animal.

* Always wash your hands after handling a pet or anything the pet has touched. Be especially careful when caring for a reptile or amphibian. They can give people a **salmonella infection**. This infection can make you very sick.

* Water is important for all pets. Clean out the water dish or bottle thoroughly. Then fill it with fresh water.

Polly Wanna Birdsit?

If you aren't used to being around birds, you'll be surprised at how smart they are! Birds like attention just like other pets.

BEFORE YOU BEGIN

Meet with your customer and the bird. Fill out a Customer Agreement form (see page 14). Write down all the details for the job.

How often will you check in on the bird?

Where is the food kept? Can you give treats to the bird?

Are there any tricks to changing its food and water? Does the bird get upset when someone reaches inside the cage?

Get the vet's name and phone number. Are there behaviors to watch out for that indicate that the bird is sick?

Learn more about pet birds. Look at the library for books on birds. Research bird care on the Internet.

ON THE JOB

* Can you let the bird out of the cage? If not, what do you do if it escapes the cage?

* If a bird doesn't know you, it might be a little scared. Talking in a calm, soothing voice will make the bird more comfortable. The bird may even chirp back a response!

Pet Bling

Each pet is special and has its own personality. Some people like **unique accessories** for their pets. If you like crafts, try making pet accessories!

WHAT YOU'LL NEED

Pet safety is important. Don't use anything sharp that could hurt the animal. Don't use anything that could be a choking hazard or be **poisonous** to the pet. Here are some ideas to get you started:

plain collars

plain bandanas

plain flying discs

stainless steel pet bowls

plain canvas bags

iron-on patches

iron

jewels

glue

stickers

non-toxic paint markers

puff and glitter paints

BEFORE YOU BEGIN

How much should you charge?

You should sell the item for more money than you spent. Here are some things to consider:

* How much did you spend on supplies?

* How long did it take you to make the item?

* What do you think people would be willing to pay?

Where can you sell your pet bling?

Your friends and family members might be good customers. You could also try some of the places below. Don't forget to get permission!

* in your front yard or the lobby of your apartment building

* at neighborhood events, such as garage sales

* at a local pet store or vet's office

DO GOOD
Donate a portion of your sales to an animal rescue organization.

Diamond Dish

Any dog or cat would be proud to have a jeweled dish. There are many sizes of bowls for big and small pets. Personalize the bowls with paint markers.

Deluxe Toy Box

Make a cool box for pet toys! Decorate it with stickers and glue-on jewels.

Bandana-Rama

Iron-on patches are a speedy way to decorate a plain bandana! Be sure to get permission to use the iron. If you've never ironed, ask for help. This is a fun way to learn!

Funky Disks

Flying disks are a favorite toy for dogs. Use non-toxic paint markers to decorate and personalize the disks.

Fancy Collars

Bling up some collars! Add colored jewels. Iron-on patches come in a lot of different designs. Paint pens or glitter puff paint can add sparkle! Try attaching cute, inexpensive charms.

Human Pooper Scooper

Meet with the customer. Fill out a Customer Agreement form (see page 14). Write down all the details for the job.

Set a **schedule**. Will you scoop every week, or just one time?

Will the customer supply bags or a trowel, or should you bring your own?

Where should you put the poop?

ON THE JOB

When you are done, be sure to wash your hands. You might want to bring hand **sanitizer**.

GO GREEN
Recycle! Save small plastic shopping bags to use for poop pick-up.

WHAT YOU'LL NEED
plastic bags

trowel or scooper

trash can

29

Tips for Success

Success isn't measured just by how much money you make. How you look and behave is also important.

BE ON TIME

Show that you are responsible and follow through on your agreements.

BE POLITE

This means that you need to respect your customer. Do not interrupt. Ask any questions politely. Be respectful even if you don't agree with someone.

DRESS FOR THE JOB

Be neat and clean, even if it's a dirty job! Wear the right clothing for the job.

BE ON THE SAFE SIDE

Follow safety instructions. Get to know the habits of the animals you care for. If a pet can go outside, make sure its leash is on before going out. Always have **emergency** contact information.

ALWAYS COMPLETE THE JOB

Remember the agreement you made? You need to follow through and do everything you agreed to do. Put away all tools and supplies you use. If you are messy or don't finish a job, you probably won't be hired again!

THIS IS JUST THE BEGINNING

Okay, it is the end of the book. But, it is just the beginning for you! This book has provided information about some ways to make money. Now decide what might work for you. Talk it over with your parents. And don't forget to have fun!

Glossary

accessory – an article of jewelry or clothing that adds completeness or attractiveness to an outfit.

discouraged – feeling that you can't do something, or that something isn't worth trying.

dispose – to get rid of something.

emergency – a sudden, unexpected, dangerous situation that requires immediate attention.

guardian – the person who, by law, cares for a minor.

infection – a disease caused by the presence of bacteria or other germs.

master – an original copy that is reproduced to make more of the same thing.

material – the substance something is made of, such as metal, fabric, or plastic.

poisonous – containing a substance that can injure or kill.

salmonella – a type of bacteria that can cause severe stomach sickness in humans and other mammals.

sanitizer – a substance that is used to kill germs.

schedule – a list of the times when things will happen.

unique – only one of its kind.

volunteer – to offer to do a job, most often without pay.

WEB SITES

To learn more about the jobs that kids can do, visit ABDO Publishing Company on the World Wide Web at www.abdopublishing.com. Web sites about creative ways for kids to earn money are featured on our Book Links page. These links are routinely monitored and updated to provide the most current information available.

Index